Original title:
The Meaning of Life (Still Looking)

Copyright © 2025 Creative Arts Management OÜ
All rights reserved.

Author: Maya Livingston
ISBN HARDBACK: 978-1-80566-172-6
ISBN PAPERBACK: 978-1-80566-467-3

Lanterns in the Mist

In the dark, lanterns sway,
Chasing shadows, night turns day.
Do they know where they're bound?
Or just twirl in merry round?

Jokes whispered by the breeze,
The moon chuckles with such ease.
Stars wink like it's all a game,
Life's a show without a name.

Each step taken, a slip or two,
Tripping over thoughts brand new.
What's the punchline? Move along,
It's all a riddle, a silly song.

With each giggle, wisdom grows,
At least that's how our story goes.
In the mist, we'll spark and shine,
Finding joy in the divine.

Dance of the Unfinished

A dance with no end in sight,
Twirling left, then taking flight.
Steps confused, but spirits high,
Laughing at the how and why.

The music plays an odd refrain,
We're lost, but it's not in vain.
Each twirl brings a brand new twist,
Who needs plans? They're overhyped!

Coffee spills on our grand plan,
A canvas life that's quite the jam.
We paint with colors wild and strange,
As the cosmos giggles at our change.

In the waltz, we take a leap,
Into the joys, both wide and deep.
Unfinished tasks? Oh, what a treat,
Here's to dancing on our feet!

Journeys through the Ether

Let's embark on flights of thought,
Whispers of wisdom, never sought.
Clouds of doubt make the trip bizarre,
But who needs a map when you've got a star?

Flying high, our wings on fire,
Life's a joke, but we won't tire.
Grab hold of laughter, spread it wide,
Through the ether, we'll take a ride.

Wrap me in nonsense, funny socks,
Time supports our paradox clocks.
Each tick-tock a silly cheer,
Life's punchline rolling ever near.

So let's sail through the absurd,
Absorb the jokes in every word.
In the ether we roam, wild and free,
Seeking joy with a side of glee.

Veils of Enigma

Behind the curtain, secrets dwell,
Odd shapes dance, casting a spell.
Is this life or a quirky dream?
With every giggle, we plot and scheme.

Veils of mystery, thick as fog,
Snoozing cats in a dialogue.
Pondering the why and how,
Clowns in the park take a bow.

Each layer peeled reveals a jest,
A puzzle where we never rest.
What's hidden beneath, we chase the light,
In shadows, we continue our flight.

So here's to the veils that tease and play,
Crafting laughter into the day.
In the enigma, let's grab a slice,
With a wink, we dance in paradise.

Footprints on Infinite Sand

I chased a wave, it laughed and swirled,
Could this be my fate, or just a twirled?
My footprints washed away, what a funny jest,
Is this the journey? Who needs the rest?

I built a castle, it crumbled with ease,
The tide's a comedian, oh how it teases!
Seagulls are squawking, what do they know?
A life's like a beach ball, just roll with the flow.

Kaleidoscope of Thoughts

My mind's like a puzzle, missing a piece,
Colorful chaos that never finds peace.
Thoughts bouncing around, like popcorn in heat,
Is this what they call a snack for the sweet?

I wonder if squirrels have it all mapped,
With acorns and giggles, they've surely been wrapped.
Life's a bright circus, don't you see?
With juggling of dreams and clowning the 'me'!

An Odyssey of Moods

I wake up as sunshine, all chipper and bright,
Then trip on a shoelace, what a strange sight!
My coffee's a jester, that spills on my shoe,
Is life really funny, or just having a screw?

Yesterday, I was a grump, like a cat in a hat,
Today, I'm a twirler, a goofy acrobat.
Emotions are marbles, rolling away,
Who's calling the shots? I'm lost in the fray.

Searching for the Unseen

I peek through foggy glasses, what's that I see?
A squirrel with a nut, laughing at me?
I search high and low for a hint and a sign,
Maybe it's hiding right under the pine!

With a map made of giggles and breadcrumbs so sweet,
I wander through fields, just me and my feet.
Perhaps life's a riddle, quite silly and grand,
Best uncovered with laughter, not plans or a brand!

Unwritten Pages of Tomorrow

In the morning I rise, my hair all a mess,
Coffee is brewing, life's little jest.
I search for the answers in my cereal bowl,
Finding deep musings in a fruity roll.

The cat walks by, judging my quest,
Paws on the keyboard like it's a test.
I scribble on napkins, my wisdom profound,
But scribbles of doodles, my thoughts turn around.

The sun starts to set, with shadows that play,
Chasing after answers that slip away.
Each wrinkle a smile, each giggle a clue,
In the puzzle of life, I'm lost but still new.

So here's to the moments, both silly and grand,
With pancakes and laughter, take life hand in hand.
While I ponder the cosmos on this fleeting ride,
I'll keep searching for meaning, with jokes as my guide.

The Elysian Enigma

Hopping through the field of forgotten thoughts,
I stumble on riddles that life never taught.
Why does my sock drawer hold all the lost,
Mates of odd shapes, at an unbearable cost?

I asked a goldfish for pearls of wise lore,
He blinked, floated 'round, then just begged for more.
The cheese in my fridge would likely agree,
That life's just a party, not meant to be spree.

With laughter as my shield, I dodge every frown,
A taco in hand, I won't drop my crown.
As time whirls around like a tumbleweed dance,
I'll twirl through the chaos, and give it a chance.

So come join my journey, it's wild and it's fun,
Grapes turn to wine, and why not make a pun?
The questions may linger, the answers may sway,
But chuckles will flutter, and brighten the day.

Kaleidoscope of Wonder

In a world of odd delights,
With socks that never match,
I chase my dreams on roller skates,
While wondering if they'll catch.

Pickles dance with jelly beans,
As squirrels play the flute,
Life's a game of hopscotch here,
With cats in tiny suits.

Tacos sing with high-pitched glee,
Chocolate rivers flow,
I wonder where the time has gone,
But then, I just don't know.

So I'll laugh and juggle lemons,
As rainbows touch the ground,
In this kaleidoscope of life,
Where joy is always found.

Unraveled Mysteries

Where did I leave my last sock?
Oh, what a funny chase!
Was it the laundry monster's fault?
Or did it sprout legs and race?

With tangled thoughts and silly dreams,
I ponder every day,
Like why does cheese and chalk not mix?
And why is there someone in my way?

As clocks go backward, cat hair flies,
And chairs begin to dance,
I sip my juice with glee and spritz,
Finding joy in every chance.

Unraveled mysteries of my life,
Inside a pizza box,
Where laughter hides with secret dreams,
And all those sneaky socks.

A Step Beyond Tomorrow

If I could hop a time machine,
What snack would I bring back?
A jelly sandwich from the dawn,
Or ice cream in a stack?

I'd laugh with folks from yesteryear,
And dance on silly tunes,
To tickle time with goofy jokes,
And sing with bouncing balloons.

With jellybeans as currency,
I'd rule this world with flair,
Issuing laughter as my coin,
Without a single care!

So let's take steps beyond today,
Into a dreamlike glow,
Where every moment's wrapped in fun,
And giggles steal the show.

The Art of Letting Go

I tossed my worries in a hat,
And watched them float away,
They danced on clouds with silly hats,
And led me on a play.

Oh, how the toaster sang to me,
While bread did somersaults,
With every cringe I let out loud,
I celebrated faults.

I waved goodbye to adulting woes,
They waved back, but who cares?
I found joy in frozen peas,
And glow-in-the-dark bears.

The art of letting go is sweet,
Like candies on a hill,
I'll keep my laughter in my heart,
And eat my find of thrill.

Lessons from the Stars

In a galaxy far and wide,
Are doubts that we all can't hide.
Stars twinkle, winking with glee,
Saying, 'Buddy, just let it be!'

Comets zoom past with a tail,
While I'm light-years slow on the trail.
Why do planets spin round and round?
Maybe they just love the sound!

Asteroids dodge like it's a dance,
And black holes? They just take a chance.
If life's a trip, let's pack some snacks,
For the cosmic route has many tracks.

A Tapestry of Questions

Threads of thought woven so tight,
Knots of wonder fill the night.
Why is pizza round in a box,
Yet we slice it into squares like socks?

Questions hang like clothes in line,
Will I ever solve the cosmic rhyme?
Do ducks think humans are strange?
Or is it us who needs the change?

Metaphors scatter like confetti,
Trying to pinpoint what's deemed heavy.
If life's a quilt, what's your patch?
Is it bright, or just a mismatch?

Footprints in the Sand

Wandering on a shore of thought,
With every step, a lesson sought.
But waves come crashing in to tease,
Erasing me with utmost ease!

Seagulls squawk like they know it all,
As I trip over a beach ball.
Is it wisdom or just a giggle?
When the waves pull in a salty wiggle?

Every grain shares a story or two,
Of epic fails and dreams anew.
So I'll stumble and laugh 'til I land,
In the whims of life, I'll make my stand!

Heartbeats of the Cosmos

If the universe has a heart,
Does it skip beats when we start?
Do stars blush when lovers gaze,
Or shudder at our clumsy phase?

Galaxies pulse with a quirky beat,
Yet here I am, stuck on repeat.
Why does a light-year take so long?
When all I want is to sing my song!

Black holes are like secrets deep,
Swallowing dreams, not a peep.
So I'll dance in nebulas bright,
Laughing at life in cosmic light!

Dancing with Questions

Why did the chicken cross the street?
To join the dance of curious feet.
With every step, a query spins,
In a twirl of giggles, where it begins.

What's the secret to happiness found?
It's buried deep in the lost and found.
With laughter as our guiding star,
We ask at least, 'Do we know who we are?'

If socks are lost, do they have fun?
Dancing alone, till the morning sun.
In this ballet of strange pursuits,
With mismatched partners, we find our roots.

When life gives lemons, we make a joke,
Witty puns with each gentle poke.
In this chaotic carnival of fate,
Let's laugh along; can't be too late!

Embrace of the Unknown

What lurks in shadows, whispers and sighs?
Is it wisdom or just a pair of flies?
In the dark, we wander and roam,
Hoping to find a welcome home.

Is that a ghost, or just my lost hair?
Every creak seems to bring a scare.
With a pillow fort as my brave retreat,
I ponder mysteries, soft and sweet.

Do clouds hold secrets, or just some rain?
Are stars just holes in a cosmic plane?
With skeptical eyes, I gaze above,
Searching for signs of life and love.

Embracing the unknown, oh what a thrill,
Each twist and turn, I embrace with skill.
With every stumble, I laugh a lot,
Maybe this crazy ride is all I've got!

Echoes of a Silent Search

Whispers echo in my head,
Are they thoughts or just crumbs of bread?
Lost in the maze of a puzzled mind,
Where every answer's a souvenir unkind.

Why do we chase ghosts in the night?
They never play fair or give us a fright.
With questions like socks, they seem to stray,
Leaving me guessing, come what may.

Who knew a rock could hold such weight?
My conscience screams, "Man, don't be late!"
Yet here I stand, still in the haze,
Tracing circles in tomorrow's maze.

In this silent search, I laugh along,
Finding absurdity in a silly song.
With a grin and a shrug, I take a leap,
Maybe the answers are just too deep!

Dreams that Lead

Do dreams have maps or secret keys?
Do they guide us through life's little sleaze?
With socks in hand and a silly hat,
I wander the paths, where's my welcome mat?

Why do we climb imaginary walls?
Just to peek behind at the laughter that calls.
Combine the flavors of joy and fright,
And taste the sweet mix of day and night.

A pizza slice in a world of regrets,
Cheesy moments, no room for debts.
In this quirky theater of the absurd,
With each pondered thought, my vision stirred.

Chasing the dreams that lead me astray,
On roller skates, I glide through the fray.
With giggles and shouts, I find my way,
In the twisty turns of a bright bouquet!

Songs of the Unattainable

I searched for gold in my cereal box,
But found only a note from a fox.
He promised me riches in a faraway land,
But first I must dance with a rubber band.

A map made of jelly, a compass of cheese,
I followed my dreams, or so I believed.
I ended up stuck in an elevator tight,
Searching for answers in the dim, flickering light.

Shards of Illumination

In a world where squirrels wear tiny hats,
I ponder the meaning while chatting with cats.
They laugh at my questions, they snicker with glee,
As I trip over thoughts that dance just like me.

A light bulb flickers, or is it a star?
I think it's a sign, but I'm not sure how far.
With each shining glimmer, I scribble my plight,
Counting my blessings—or was that a bite?

Grassroots of Wonder

On a quest for the tasty, I climbed a tall tree,
Searching for wisdom in a hive of bees.
They buzzed me a riddle with honey-soaked care,
I left with some laughter and a beehive hair.

The ground shook with giggles from flowers so bright,
They whispered their secrets under the moonlight.
I learned that the land of the curious dream,
Is sprinkled with sprinkles and topped with whipped cream.

Within the Canvas of Time

I painted my worries on canvas so wide,
But the colors ran off for a playful hide.
With each stroke that faltered, I chuckled aloud,
As my masterpiece turned into a circus crowd.

The hours, they giggle; they slip through my hands,
Like grains of fine sand that escape my plans.
I ponder the moments wrapped in a rhyme,
And laugh as I fumble within the canvas of time.

Whispers of Existence

In a world where socks disappear,
We chase our dreams without much fear.
Cats plot schemes, fish swim around,
Life's just a circus, a playful sound.

Balloons float high, cupcakes abound,
We ponder if happiness can be found.
Coffee spills, laughter fills the air,
What's the secret? Do we even care?

So we dance like no one's watching here,
While ice cream melts down our chin with cheer.
With each goofy step, we take a glance,
At life's quirky rhythm, a funny dance.

As we giggle at our silly plight,
Isn't confusion a pure delight?
Chasing rainbows, we might not see,
That life's a joke, served with some glee.

Searching Shadows

Under streetlights, shadows play,
Chasing dreams that run away.
Lost in thoughts, we take a stroll,
Is there a map to find our goal?

We search for answers in a pie,
Daredevil squirrels shoot for the sky.
With each tumble, we laugh and roll,
Life's a riddle without a toll.

Beneath the surface, whispers reside,
Where lost keys and good times collide.
Grab your snacks, it's time to roam,
Let's explore the great unknown home.

In a world where questions are absurd,
Finding meaning can feel unheard.
Yet with a wink and a playful grin,
We'll toast to chaos as our win.

Echoes of Purpose

In the coffee shop, dreams take flight,
As we ponder and scribble what's right.
Spilling thoughts like beans on the floor,
Are we destined to search for more?

Traffic lights twinkle with cheeky flair,
While pigeons plot with a bold, blank stare.
Life's just a sitcom with a hint of spice,
Juggling regrets like a bowl of rice.

Peeking through clouds, a smile appears,
Formulas break over hearty cheers.
As we trip on thoughts, laughter prevails,
We sail on bold, unfading trails.

In each tumbling moment, we lean and sway,
Finding humor in life's wild ballet.
So let's toast to the absurd and strange,
In our playful antics, we will arrange.

Threads of Tomorrow

With a tap dance on the kitchen floor,
We knit our dreams, stitch by stitch, more.
Laughter flutters like a gentle breeze,
Unraveling mysteries with playful tease.

Knitting needles click, creating a trend,
As puppy eyes watch us laugh and pretend.
Each loop a question, each purl a thought,
In this quirky universe, we're blissfully caught.

The clock ticks slowly, a giggling thief,
What if the answer is just relief?
In the bumpy road of life's parade,
There are more jokes here than hopes betrayed.

So let's follow the laughter, not just the signs,
In this tapestry, there are no confines.
With every twist, we're bound to find,
A silly embrace of the curious mind.

Finding Solace in the Chaos

In a world that spins so fast,
I trip on things that never last.
The coffee spills, the cat does zoom,
Is it laughter or just doom?

I search for peace in cereal boxes,
While dodging life's relentless foxes.
Reality's a chuckle and a poke,
Like finding joy in a big fat yolk.

I dance with socks upon the floor,
And twirl 'round like I'm at a store.
Each misstep a glittering prize,
While neighbors watch with widened eyes.

So here's to chaos, let it reign,
Each silly stumble brings some gain.
I'll laugh and giggle 'til I drop,
This jumbled ride will never stop.

Whispering to the Void

I stood and whispered to the air,
'Tell me, void, why are you there?'
It shrugged and sent a breeze my way,
Said 'Life's a game, come out to play!'

Chasing shadows, I trip on light,
And serenade the stars at night.
Each cosmic wink a little joke,
As I ponder if I'm really woke.

The toaster burns my morning bread,
A sign that fate is somewhat fed.
I chuckle as I scrape away,
Wondering what lives might sway.

In this void, we dance and spin,
Unraveling where dreams begin.
With every question, laugh, and cheer,
The void just giggles, oh so near.

Whispers of Existence

I caught a butterfly with a net,
It laughed and said, 'You caught a pet!'
I shrugged and sighed, 'But what's its name?'
It fluttered off, no sense of shame.

Existence plays like hide and seek,
With answers ticking, ever meek.
I ask the fridge, it hums a tune,
While dancing 'neath the lazy moon.

I tried to count the stars so bright,
Got lost mid-way—now that's my plight!
Each twinkling laugh a gentle tease,
In cosmic games, I beg and plead.

The joy of wandering through the day,
Is finding smiles along the way.
Through whispers soft and giggles loud,
Existence dances, free and proud.

Echoes in the Void

I shouted loud into the night,
The echo chuckled, 'What a fright!'
With every bounce, it changed its tone,
As if the void made friends alone.

I searched for wisdom in a shoe,
Found nothing but a flower too.
My thoughts went bowling with a twist,
A funny strike I won't resist.

The universe plays hide and seek,
With winking stars and moons that leak.
Each pondered thought a bouncy ball,
Into the void where giggles call.

So let us shout, then laugh some more,
Into the void, let spirits soar.
With echoes playful in the night,
Life's a jest, and what a sight!

Ciphers of Being

Why do socks vanish, where do they flee?
Is it a secret, for you and for me?
The cat's on a mission, plotting a scheme,
To decode our lives while we all just dream.

Is pizza a snack or a culinary quest?
Can chocolate be deemed as a form of rest?
These puzzles perplex us, we scratch our heads,
Searching for truths where the logic treads.

Do goldfish ponder their watery fate?
Or plot grand escapes from their glassy state?
In this funhouse mirror, we laugh and we cry,
As meaning dances just out of our eye.

Perhaps life's a riddle, or merely a game,
With dice always rolling, but no one to blame.
So let's toast to nonsense, toast to our fears,
With plenty of laughter, and maybe some beers.

Chasing Elusive Rainbows

Who knew that rainbows were slippery guys?
Chasing their colors is filled with surprise.
Where do they end? What's their glorious goal?
Perhaps it's a pot of pure jelly roll!

Why do we think there's a treasure up there?
When all that we find is some cold, damp air?
With leprechauns laughing and making us chase,
We skip and we hop, yet they're gone without trace.

The moon looks so close, yet it's far from our reach,
Is it hiding a lesson, some wisdom to teach?
We clutch at the stars like a kid with a toy,
As we wonder and giggle, both grave and coy.

So dance in the puddles, wear mismatched socks,
Life's a confetti of giggles and knocks.
In chasing those rainbows, we might just find,
The jokes that we chase are not what defined.

A Tapestry Unwoven

Life's like a quilt that someone forgot,
Each piece a puzzle, each patch a thought.
With mismatched fabric and random designs,
It's cozy and warm, yet it seldom aligns.

Grandma once told me, "What's wrong with a stitch?
A life full of chaos can still be a rich!"
So here are the threads, frayed, loose, and bright,
We sew up our joys as we laugh through the night.

Why do we measure our worth by the yard?
Some patches have polka dots, others are marred.
Yet in this wild weave, there's beauty abound,
With each tangled thread, a new laugh can be found.

So let's put away rulers, let go of our qualms,
Embrace all the shambles, the giggles, the charms.
For in every loose fiber, every wild seam,
Rests the essence of living, of laughter, of dream.

Beyond the Veil of Now

Time's a magician, it pulls us along,
One minute I'm here, next I'm missing the gong.
With clocks that tick-tock like a chorus of frogs,
We're stuck in a traffic jam jammed with old dogs.

Worrying 'bout tomorrows, while yesterday's cool,
We juggle our moments, but who made the rules?
When life's a parade with a clown who just slips,
"Do I take a left, or a ride on the ships?"

So let's toss out our planners, embrace the unknown,
With muffins of madness and wild hopes we've sewn.
In laughter we'll find what tomorrow may bring,
The magic behind, and the joy in the swing.

What if the secret is simple and free?
Tap dance on stardust, my friend, and just be.
With folly and laughter, the moments will grow,
For life is a play that we all get to show.

Quest for Clarity

In a world of confusion, I try to unwind,
Chasing answers elusive, a riddle unkind.
With a scoop of good humor and a sprinkle of grace,
I wander through life at a comical pace.

I asked a wise owl, perched high in a tree,
"What's the secret to laughter? Please share it with me!"
He hooted and chuckled, then flew off in a twirl,
Leaving me pondering like a forgetful squirrel.

I searched high and low for that pearl of a thought,
But found mostly trip-ups and lessons long taught.
With every wrong turn, I could feel my hair frizz,
Yet I giggled and danced, saying, "What a fine whiz!"

Now I scribble my feelings on crumpled up napkins,
If the universe answers, I might pop like a daffodil.
But if it just chuckles, I'll laugh right along,
In this grand little quest, I have never felt wrong.

Reflections in the Silence

In the quiet of night, I ponder and sigh,
Stars look like winks—from my blanket, I'll fly.
What's the purpose of dancing in circles, I think?
Maybe it's just to find the right kind of drink!

I met a wise tortoise who spoke with delight,
"Life's like a bagel, it's round and it's bright.
Sometimes you get cream cheese, sometimes bare bread,
But the crunch in each bite? It's something!" he said.

I practiced my yoga while sardines jumped high,
Contorting my body, I thought, "Oh my, why?"
The meaning, I mused, was as slippery as soap,
In that twist and that turn, I'd still find my hope.

So I gather my giggles, my grumbles, my cheers,
These reflections in silence turn whispers to years.
Finding humor in moments, I'll twirl without care,
For life's just a riddle, and I'm glad I'm aware!

Beyond the Horizon

I gazed at the sunset with chips in my hand,
Wishing for wisdom—no map, just a plan.
What lies beyond that great fiery ball?
A bar where the laughs never seem to stall!

I asked a tall cactus with googly eyes,
"Hey, do you think I might get some surprise?"
He shrugged with a prick and said, "Just look around,
Life's quirkiest truths can be easily found."

So I hopped on my bike, with a grin on my face,
Scouring the hills for my next funny place.
But all I found were some sheep in a race,
With woofery bleats they demanded some grace.

I laughed 'til I cried, at the silliness here,
Maybe life's essence is wrapped up in cheer.
Beyond every horizon, new giggles unfold,
I'll chase them forever, for laughter is gold!

Chasing Fleeting Moments

I stroll through the park, my thoughts on the run,
Chasing those moments that vanish like sun.
Like squirrels with a plan, they scamper away,
Life says, "Catch me quick, or I'll make you okay!"

A dog in a tutu ran past with a bark,
While I pondered my shoes—their laces so dark.
What's this little game, is it supposed to be fun?
It seems sheer absurdity has already begun!

With bubbles and giggles floating all around,
I found that the small things make joy truly abound.
From ice cream cones melting to rain on the ground,
Fleeting moments are silly, and happily drowned.

So I'll keep on chasing, despite all the frowns,
Through tickles and grins, through jewels and through crowns.
For in every quick smile, I capture a glimpse,
That life's just a circus, and I'm dancing with imps!

The Unwritten Path

I stumbled on my morning walk,
With coffee in my hand, I talk.
The birds all watch with judging eyes,
As I trip over my own shoe ties.

The sidewalk's cracked, it feels like fate,
Yet I still ponder, 'Am I too late?'
A squirrel stops to give a stare,
Maybe it knows why I'm not sure where.

I chase my dreams through crow and crow,
But they just caw, and then they go.
Each step is random, full of glee,
Is this the best path? Well, we'll see!

Should I ask the grass for advice,
Or consult the clouds? Oh, that's nice!
But they just laugh and puff away,
Maybe I'll wing it every day.

Embracing the Unknown

I'm here with gum on my old shoe,
Why's this journey so hard to chew?
A map? No thanks, I'll just pretend,
That every corner's a brand-new trend.

I booked a flight to who-knows-where,
And packed my socks, a wild affair.
The pilot grinned, said, 'Hold on tight!'
I shrugged and thought, 'This feels just right.'

The snacks are good aboard this trip,
Though my heart might occasionally skip.
Each mile I leap, the more I cringe,
But isn't that why we all binge?

Strange faces smile, they greet me kind,
In oddest crowds, true friends I find.
So here's to life, as wild as this,
Who needs a plan when chaos is bliss?

Fragments of Forever

I gathered memories like lost socks,
The ones that hide in closet blocks.
A rubber band, an old receipt,
Sure hold the secrets of my heartbeat.

I scribble notes on napkins worn,
Each dream is tossed, and I am torn.
A dance with time, a silly spin,
What was I doing? Where to begin?

I met a cat who spoke in rhyme,
"Your worries, my friend, are simply sublime!"
So I laughed, discarded my old fears,
And wheeled my suitcase through the years.

Each fragment shines in its own way,
Brightening up the dullest day.
So here I am, with socks that fade,
What meaning comes from this parade?

Dance of the Uncertain

I waltzed with doubt on Tuesday night,
My left foot's heavy, the right just might.
With every step, I twist and turn,
Why is this dance a lesson learned?

The DJ spins my dreams on track,
Confetti falls, I'll never look back.
A partner trips and laughs so loud,
At least together, we're awkwardly proud.

The spotlight shines, it brings a glow,
But do I lead? Not sure, you know.
We spin and swing, a random blast,
Who knew this dance could go by fast?

So here we twirl, through life's routine,
Embracing all, and vibes unseen.
And if I fall, I'll just laugh it through,
Life's just a dance, with friends like you.

Verse of the Unknown

Why do we dance in the rain, you ask?
As we stumble through puddles, what a task!
Searching for wisdom among the socks,
Well, perhaps it's just time for some fun talks!

Do we ponder life over breakfast fries?
With ketchup as our sage and toast as our prize?
Between sips of coffee, dreams start to sprout,
Knowing life's questions give laughter a shout!

We wear our hats, each one a disguise,
As the cat tries to ponder in muted cries.
The answer might hide in your left shoe's sole,
Or maybe it's stuck in that never-read scroll!

So grab your thoughts, let's make a parade,
Life's mysteries tackled, let's not be afraid.
We're all silly poets with light in our eyes,
Chasing the unknown like mischievous spies!

Seasons of Reflection

Spring brings blossoms and questions anew,
While winter hints 'Why are you so blue?'
Fall leaves whisper secrets, they spin and twirl,
As summer's sun laughs, creating a whirl!

In spring, we frolic with ducks at the pond,
While pondering if this day is the one we abscond.
Each season unfolds like a taco surprise,
With guacamole wisdom and piquant goodbyes!

Summer cookouts serve warmth on a plate,
While ants just march in, but who can hate?
Do they have a plan, or just follow the line?
While we munch on chips, life seems pretty fine!

Oh autumn, your leaves make us ponder too deep,
Should we rake them up or let nature just keep?
And in winter, hot cocoa warms questions like frost,
Is pondering life just a game we all lost?

Echoes of the Eternal Quest

I once sought a sage with feathers and flair,
His knowledge was sprinkled, but he just sat there.
He said, 'Ask an octopus, it's smarter than me,'
So I went searching in the deep, blue sea!

Yet the octopus whispered from its coral lair,
'Life's like a taco, flavors are rare!'
And I giggled at wisdom from tentacles wise,
Finding truth is just messy like sweet, sweet pies.

Next, I met a dog with a tail made of dreams,
He barked out revelations amidst squeaky screams.
Chasing after thoughts, he raced through the grass,
In pursuit of delivery, with questions amassed!

So I joined the chase, what fun it would be,
From barking and laughing! Oh, life's such a spree.
In echoes resounding, we find joy we request,
As we dance through existence, that playful jest!

Masks of Perception

We wear our masks, a clown and a sage,
Why so serious? Turn that page!
Life's a carnival, each twist a delight,
With mischief and giggles beneath the moonlight!

Yet sometimes, a question likes to creep in,
'What's the punchline?' Oh, let's begin!
With donuts and laughter, we ponder the same,
As mime artists dance in this ridiculous game.

The wise owl squawks, 'Life's not so clear,'
I reply, 'But that's why the fun's here!'
We juggle our worries, with pies in the air,
In this circus of puzzling, we all freely share!

So grab a balloon, let's float through the show,
With each heartfelt laugh, we just let it flow.
In the masks that we wear, laughter's the key,
With whimsical wonders, we can always be free!

Fables of Forgotten Dreams

In a land where socks go to roam,
A tale of lost hopes found a home.
Chasing rainbows in a paper boat,
  Singing off-key, note for note.

A chicken crossed the road for a snack,
With dreams of gold and a second act.
In the end, all it found was a fry,
  And thought, 'Hey, at least I can fly!'

A Flicker in the Void

Stars twinkle like my late-night snacks,
Winking softly; they've got no tracks.
I ponder on planets, all shiny and round,
While searching for meaning that can't be found.

A cow jumped high to kiss the moon,
Wishing on wishes like the world's a cartoon.
In a dance of gravity, it stumbled and fell,
And said, 'This round world? It's quite a hard sell!'

Touching the Infinite

There once lived a cat with a curious tail,
It chased its own shadow, set out on a trail.
With each wild leap, it pounced on a dream,
Thinking, 'Maybe I'm part of a scheme!'

Frogs in tuxedos hopped high for the show,
Debating if life was just all for the dough.
They chuckled and croaked through the muck and the mire,
As the world spun around on an electric wire.

Hues of Transience

A painter once mixed colors of glee,
Swirling in circles, as bright as can be.
But the hues all giggled, they jumped off the page,
Declaring, 'Life's a bright, silly stage!'

In a kitchen where cooks never cease,
A recipe said, 'Your soul's a piece.'
But the spoon just jiggled and danced with delight,
Saying, 'I'm just here for a sprinkle of spice!'

Puzzles of Reality

Life's a jigsaw, pieces askew,
Where's the corner? No hint, no clue.
Cats and dogs play in my mind,
Chasing tails, leaving sense blind.

Balloons float high in the sky,
One popped—oh me, oh my!
Is joy just a joke from a clown?
Or is it that we all wear a frown?

Ticklish thoughts bounce in my head,
Like rubber chickens, always misled.
Questions swirling like a dance,
In this circus, we prance and glance.

So let's eat cake, wear funny hats,
While pondering life's silly spats.
Could truth hide in a joke so plain?
Maybe laughter drowns all the pain.

Wandering through Time

Days tick by like an old clock's chime,
Who stole my youth? Was it a crime?
I lost my keys, but found my socks,
Life's a riddle inside a box.

Goblins grin in the rearview lens,
Did they pay tolls? Oh, the suspense!
Each twist and turn a plot so wild,
Like a toddler's tantrum, unbeguiled.

Socks twice matched, but scars still show,
Time's a prankster, don't you know?
We run in circles, it's quite absurd,
Chasing wisdom like a lost bird.

So hop on a train, grab a snack,
Can't miss a moment—there's no going back.
Embrace the detours, those paths unworn,
In this comedy, we're reborn.

Notes from a Forgotten Road

Maps mislead, like dreams in the fog,
Did I just step in something? A dog?
Wandered left, took a wrong turn,
Can't find the way, but oh how I yearn.

Scribbled notes on a crumpled sheet,
"Turn right at the street with the treat."
But lo and behold, I see no shop,
Just a squirrel doing a funny hop.

Each bend could lead to a land of sweets,
Or tangled vines with mischievous beats.
Adventure calls, my heart does race,
In life's mishmash, I find my place.

So I'll whistle loud, embrace the chance,
With every wrong path, there's time to dance.
In the chaos, joy I'll unearth,
Finding laughter is what I'm worth.

Reflections in a Broken Mirror

Glimmers of me in shards of glass,
Smiling face that's sure to pass.
Painted clown with a silly grin,
What's behind this messy skin?

Each crack a story, a whispered jest,
Life's too funny not to jest.
Wigs and mustaches, all in play,
In this funhouse, I'll find my way.

Riddles dance in reflections grand,
Plucking at thoughts like a band.
What's real, what's fake? A paradox,
Like trying to tickle a box of rocks.

So let's toast to the clowns while we cheer,
Life's a joke? Well, grab a beer!
In broken glam, we find our cheer—
Laughter is the best souvenir.

Beyond the Horizon

I peeked beyond the curtain bright,
To find my socks in a silly fight.
They argued over who was worn last,
While I just laughed, my day was vast.

A cheese-shaped moon began to glow,
I pondered on where the lost socks go.
Perhaps they dance in fields of cheese,
Or sail on ships with the greatest ease.

My cat sat plotting his next big dream,
To catch a bird or maybe a beam.
He missed the fly that buzzed right near,
Life's just one laugh and a tinge of cheer.

So here's a toast to silly sights,
To socks that dance and moonlit nights.
For in the chase, we often find,
Laughter and joy, our hearts unwind.

Dreams Without Borders

In a land where waffles grow on trees,
I ponder my lunch as my stomach pleads.
With syrup rivers and buttered hills,
I'll conquer breakfast, oh what thrills!

My dreams are stuck in a traffic jam,
With burgers and fries, oh, what a scam!
I see my wishes in a fast-food line,
And wonder if pickles think they're divine.

What if my dreams had little wings?
Would they learn to dance and do silly things?
A waltz with donuts, a jig with pie,
Life's just absurd, so why not try?

So I'll skip through life in sparkly shoes,
Collecting all laughter, I just can't lose.
With every hiccup and goofy fall,
I find the fun, oh, that's the call.

Tides of Uncertainty

The waves crashed in with a cheesy grin,
As I tried to surf, but fell in the fin.
A seagull laughed, dropped a fish on my head,
I wondered if life was just being misled.

The sands did tickle my toes so fleet,
While crabs wore sunglasses, looking quite neat.
I pondered my purpose between each splash,
As the tide rolled in with a carefree clash.

What if the jellyfish danced to a beat?
Would life be sweeter, or just more neat?
A conga line of fish in a shy little school,
Reminds me that fun can be the best tool.

So here by the ocean, I'll play and I'll sway,
With all of the creatures, we'll brighten the day.
In the dance of the tides, I find my delight,
And giggle through life, 'til morning's first light.

Stories Yet Untold

In my closet, a dragon snores,
Wearing pajamas, he dreams of chores.
He wants to tidy and sweep the floor,
But I'd rather have fun and explore!

The books on the shelf hold tales so grand,
Of pirates at sea and a talking hand.
If only they'd speak, oh what would they say?
Perhaps they'd suggest we all go play!

Every sock has a story, or so they claim,
Of great adventures and a sock puppet fame.
With mismatched friends saying silly things,
They teach me how joy, like humor, springs.

So I'll spin fibs of my cat on a quest,
Who battles the vacuum, he thinks he's the best.
With laughter as ink, I write my own scrolls,
For in every chuckle, my heart surely rolls.

A Pathless Journey

I wandered through the hall of doubt,
With a signpost saying, 'Turn about!'
My coffee spills, I trip and squeal,
   Is clarity some sort of deal?

My GPS says, 'Just keep it cool,'
But I lost my phone, what a fool!
I dance with questions, twirl in delight,
Should I chase the moon or hug the night?

Amidst the trees, with squirrels I speak,
  They nod their heads, but never peak.
A pathless journey, wild and free,
With laughter, I just might find me!

So here I am with thoughts askew,
   In silly shoes, a life's debut.
I might not know just where to go,
But I skip along, and steal the show!

The Art of Inquiry

Why is the sky a shade of blue?
Is that a rabbit in my stew?
With questions stacked like pancakes high,
I wonder if the moon gets shy.

I ask the sun about its glow,
It chuckles back, 'Just take it slow!'
A talking cloud just passed me by,
It said, 'Don't fret, just ask why!'

Inquirers hold a special place,
With silly hats, we lead the chase.
We seek the truth beneath the guise,
But mostly we just improvise!

So if you ponder, stop, and smile,
Embrace the questions with your style.
In every 'what' and 'how' we find,
The art of inquiry, oh so kind!

Circles of Uncertainty

Round and round, the questions spin,
Am I losing or just chagrined?
A circle dance of joy and dread,
Where'd I put my common thread?

I tried to square this problematic chase,
But ended up in a lopsided place.
With giggles echoing in my ears,
I embrace the chaos with my cheers!

What if the fish just wants to sing?
Or if the cat knows everything?
In circles, we joke and trade a smile,
Uncertainty can be quite worthwhile!

So spin around, let laughter flow,
In every twist, there's room to grow.
The world's a stage, we're all in tune,
In circles of doubt, we dance 'til noon!

The Fleeting Glimpse

A glimpse of wisdom, quick as flash,
I craved the truth, but got a splash!
With rubber ducks and dancing bees,
I ponder life by giant trees.

A fleeting thought just raced by me,
Wearing a hat that was quite funky.
It whispered low, 'Just have some fun,'
Life's riddles work when you're on the run!

With giggles shared and pies on plates,
Every second's rich, so don't be late!
Grab that wink, don't let it fade,
The fleeting glimpse is how it's made!

In every chuckle and silly jest,
We find the clues, we're truly blessed.
So let your heart soar and take that leap,
In fleeting moments, joys run deep!

Symphony of Unanswered Queries

Why do socks go missing, my friend?
Do they dance with the dust bunnies till the end?
Is our fate decided by a flip of a coin?
Or by pizza toppings we choose to run on?

Every stray cat knows more than we think,
While we ponder our coffee with a sip and a wink.
Is the purpose to find out which movies to binge?
Or the sweetness of chocolate, how much we can cringe?

The stars are just dots in the vast cosmic game,
Yet they sparkle and twinkle, igniting our flame.
As we chase our own tails in this crazy ol' show,
Laughing with strangers, where does this all go?

With questions in pockets and hearts full of cheer,
We'll sip on our doubts, add a splash of our fear.
The answers escape like soap bubbles in air,
Yet we're all just a bit too lost to care!

Beyond the Last Sunset

As I gaze at the sky, what do I truly seek?
An answer more profound or a taco this week?
Do dreams float on clouds or do they just stray?
Fading like daylight in a humorous way.

Maybe life's just a joke, played for a laugh,
With punchlines appearing as we stumble and gaffe.
Is the goal to collect all the world's flavors?
Or just pet the cats that inspire our labors?

Yet, what if the end is a pizza party?
With toppings as wisdom, all shared with the hearty.
While we dance with the stars, let's pull up a chair,
And toast to our queries - let's not lose our flair!

So I wander with giggles, and a slice in my hand,
In this riddle of life, let laughter expand.
For what's at the finish, we may never know,
But a chuckle and two pies sounds good in this flow!

Fragments of an Elusive Path

Wearing mismatched shoes, I set off on my quest,
With breadcrumbs of hopes that I made as a jest.
Do we chase butterflies or a fleeting dream?
Or maybe just ice cream, oh how they gleam!

Each stumble, a giggle, each fall, a delight,
As I dance with my shadow, a silly sight.
Are we meant to conquer the mountains we climb?
Or sip sunlit moments, one sip at a time?

Perhaps I should ask the old tree on the way,
It chuckles and rustles, what wisdom today?
Stuck between branches, where secrets reside,
Could laughter unlock the door to a glide?

With pockets full of laughter, and maps made of dreams,
I'll wander this path with my unwieldy schemes.
Each question I carry like birds on a spree,
In the dance of existence, it's all just for me!

Weight of the Unexplained

Is life just a puzzle with pieces misplaced?
Like socks hiding under chairs – now that's a good taste!
Do we shine like the stars or just glow with a grin?
Laughing at mysteries we can't keep in.

Each morning's a riddle, the coffee's way strong,
As I search for the meaning in a ketchup song.
Can the universe hear our mumblings and schemes?
Or is it like background music in our wild dreams?

With questions unending, I wear a big hat,
Should I dance in the rain, or just stay and chat?
For every 'why' tossed out, there's a chuckle to find,
In this circus of chaos, we all are aligned.

So here's to the questions, let's raise up a toast!
For laughter's the answer we cherish the most.
As we wander through wonders and laugh at the night,
Embracing the weight as we chase our own light!

Questions Beneath the Surface

Why is pizza round but served in a square?
And socks mysteriously vanish, do they really care?
Do fish get thirsty, or just swim with glee?
Are clouds the pillows where dreams float free?

Why do we buy whole melons, just to get a slice?
And what's with all this wisdom that comes at a price?
Is time a river, or just a trick of the eye?
If we're all just passing through, why don't we fly?

Do plants chat softly when the sun dips low?
And do ants have meetings, oh what do they know?
When does laughter become a secret code?
As we wander on this endless road?

Should I chase the stars or settle for a snack?
Is fun a compass, or just a quirky knack?
In this grand circus, we're all a bit odd,
So smile and wonder, it's a playful façade.

Labyrinths of the Heart

Why do we fall for hearts with strange little quirks?
Like the one who thought pants were just a lot of works.
Do we trade these hearts like trading cards at school?
Or are they more precious than any silly jewel?

In this maze of emotions, do we take lots of turns?
With lessons like fire, is it passion that burns?
Can love be a noodle, all twisted and bent?
Or shall we just laugh—a jolly event?

Why do texts go unread, like secrets stuck in time?
Is silence a language, or just a bad rhyme?
Do we play hide-and-seek with our feelings so bright?
Or swim in confusion, deep into the night?

With every lost blush, did we learn how to play?
In this game of affection, do we just find our way?
So let's dance in circles and twirl in delight,
For every heart's labyrinth has its own light.

Sifting Through Sand

Life's like a beach, do I dig for the shells?
Or just build a castle, and see how it dwells?
Do grains hold the secrets of time's endless roll?
Or are they just whispers, all part of the whole?

While looking for treasures, I trip on a rock,
Should I gather the gold, or just chill and talk?
Why's the sun so hot, but the ocean's so cool?
Is it all one big game, or did I miss the school?

Do the waves have a rhythm, or dance like we do?
Are tides just the ocean's moody issues?
As I sift through the sand, does wisdom slip by?
Or is it just laughter that helps me get by?

Let's trade all our stories, like marbles held tight,
For the joy in the searching makes everything bright.
So grab a handful of sand and let it all flow,
In this quirky adventure, there's so much to know.

Flickers of Truth

Do fireflies ponder on the meaning of light?
Or do they just flicker, all merry at night?
Is truth like a pickle—tangy and bold?
Or a slippery fish that can never be sold?

In the search for real answers, do we swap our tales?
With a wink and a grin, are we spinning our sails?
Is the universe laughing, or just playing pretend?
Or is time a swap meet where every truth bends?

Is honesty just a puzzle missing some pieces?
Or a pie in the oven that slowly releases?
Do laughs hold the answers to questions we seek?
Or are they just echoes that play hide-and-seek?

Let's shimmer like stars while we giggle and ponder,
As we chase the bright secrets, like kids full of wonder.
In the game of existence, find joy in the slight,
For we're all just here up to our ears in the light.

Mosaic of Thoughts

In a world of colorful tiles,
I search for the truth in my smiles.
Each piece is a laugh, a silly glance,
Creating a picture of life's strange dance.

I trip over dreams, they'd rather not stay,
Like socks in the wash, all lost in the fray.
Sipping on coffee, I ponder the fate,
Of socks and of dreams and of lunch on my plate.

Puzzles unfold, like socks on the floor,
Life plays its tricks, oh, who could want more?
I chase after meaning, it hops like a flea,
Like a cat in the sun, it just won't sit free.

Yet here in this chaos, I find joy to claim,
In laughter and mishaps, there's fun in the game.
So here's to the tiles, both bright and absurd,
Together they make up the song of the world.

Foraging for Clarity

With a basket in hand, I roam through the mess,
Foraging for clarity, trying to guess.
Each fruit that I find, a topic to chew,
Some sweet, some quite sour, just like my view.

I dodge all the nonsense, I hop over fears,
Searching for laughter, for moments that cheers.
Nature's a buffet, so tasty, divine,
Yet somehow I end up with pickles and brine.

I nibble on dreams, while dodging the doubts,
They whisper in shadows, they linger, they flout.
But joy is the harvest I gather each day,
In quirky little nuggets, come what may.

So I'll feast on the funny, skip bland carefully,
For clarity's a dish served ironically.
And here in this kitchen of whimsical strife,
I slice through the chaos — hey, that's just life!

Light in the Abyss

In caverns of gray, where shadows do play,
I search for a spark to brighten my day.
With a headlamp of laughter, I dance in the gloom,
Painting all darkness with jokes that consume.

I tumble and fumble, a klutz in the night,
Falling for humor, it feels just so right.
Exploring the depths, I find it a hit,
Every stumble a giggle, every trip a skit.

Down here in the depths, the echoes do sing,
Of puns and of myths and the joy that they bring.
A twinkle of nonsense, a prank on the heart,
In the light of the abyss, laughter's an art.

So let shadows be friends, let them play on my skin,
For each quirk and each twist is where life can begin.
In caverns of humor, my fears fade to mist,
A light in the abyss — how could I resist?

Quest for the Next Tear

With scrolls in my pocket, I fantasize grand,
A quest for the next tear, a place I can stand.
Wiping a chuckle away, just in case,
I stumble on joy while I search for a place.

Each tear is a gem, a laugh crystal clear,
Like slipping on bananaskin, things can endear.
Expectations are silly, they slip from my grasp,
The journey for laughter is often a gasp.

I track all the puns down, like treats in a maze,
With paths that twist wildly, oh what a craze!
Each giggle, a marker, each snort, a delight,
A map drawn in laughter, where day plays with night.

So here's my adventure, my wild little plea,
For giggles and chuckles, they nourish me.
In tears that I search for, a joy will shine through,
If life is a quest, then I quest just for you.

Flickering Flame of Hope

In a world of endless quests,
With questions stacked like weird requests,
I search for wisdom, like a gnome,
Yet trip over socks instead of a tome.

Each clue I find's a playful jest,
It seems even ducks don't know the rest,
I ponder while tied up in lace,
Is this the path or a shoe-tying race?

They say to live is to seek a sign,
But all I find is a flatline spine,
So I dance with squirrels, oh what a sight,
Laughing, I wonder if they get it right.

My coffee spills while my thoughts swirl,
Like a lost boy in a candy pearl,
Each sip a puzzle, each laugh a clue,
Still searching for meaning, or maybe a zoo.

Notes from an Unfinished Symphony

Like a cat trying to play the lute,
I strum a tune, but it sounds quite brute,
Each note I hit is a question mark,
A serenade sung in the dark.

Life plays on, a crazy refrain,
With offbeat rhythms driving me insane,
Do I follow the melody's lead?
Or just enjoy the dance of the weed?

Each stumble's a step toward the grand design,
Yet my shoes don't match, and I need some wine,
I wrote a sonnet on a napkin, true,
But it vanished like my morning brew.

The orchestra plays, I can't find my cue,
So I pop like popcorn, it's all I can do,
An unfinished tune, a hapless quest,
With laughter as my final jest.

Colors of the Unseen

I paint my thoughts in colors bright,
But magic markers run from fright,
The greenish hue of doubt and fear,
A canvas filled with laughter here.

I mix emotions in a funky bowl,
Like a chef who lost his sense of goal,
Each brushstroke leads to silly shapes,
Like ducks in hats or wooly capes.

The blue of calm, the red of glee,
Deep purple whispers, 'Just be free!'
Yet still I wonder, where's the light?
Oh look, a pinwheel! It's taken flight!

The unseen colors, they sing and sway,
In this art class, I lost my way,
A joyful mismatch, a playful spree,
Life's an odd painting, just let it be.

The Journey Within

I embarked on a quest to find my soul,
But got stuck in a bowl of guacamole,
Thoughts rolled away like marbles at night,
Have I found myself? Well, not quite right.

Maps of my heart are riddled with fries,
Where's the treasure? It's under my eyes,
I rummage through dreams like a child with toys,
But all I find are some fluffy noise.

In the depths of my mind, a sock puppet reigns,
Spouting wisdom through its cotton veins,
It's ruffled yet true, oh, what a find!
Perhaps I'm just lost, with snacks in my mind!

So I'll keep searching, with giggles and grace,
Through tangled thoughts, I'll chase this race,
A journey within, with a laugh so bright,
Life's a messy dance, oh what a fright!

Navigating the Abyss

In search of wisdom, lost my keys,
Life's a riddle, like bloated cheese.
I follow signs that lead to snacks,
Finding truth in late-night hacks.

I danced with shadows, tripped on fate,
A clown's routine, it's all first rate.
The mirror laughs, I'm not quite right,
But hey, I shine, though not so bright.

Questions swirl like leaves in wind,
My goldfish knows more, I rescind.
I scribble thoughts on napkin scraps,
While pondering all my mishaps.

So here's a toast to wobbling dreams,
Life's not perfect, or so it seems.
With a grin, I'll take a dive,
In this slippery, twisted jive.

Lanterns in the Dark

I tripped over wisdom in the night,
Sent my thoughts into blind flight.
Like lanterns bobbing on the sea,
Each flicker giggles back at me.

Darkness teases with silly pranks,
I find my way through misfit ranks.
Lost in puzzles, worn-out shoes,
Still, I dance to my own blues.

The shadows whisper silly tales,
Of mismatched socks and drunken snails.
I chase reflections down the street,
Where laughter-echoes play their beat.

Guide me home, my lantern bright,
Through the chaos of the night.
With a wink and nod, I play along,
In this goofy, cosmic song.

Mosaic of Dreams

In a patchwork quilt of cosmic fun,
I stick my head in a toaster's run.
Trying to find where the cupcakes are,
In this dreamy dance, how bizarre!

Crumbs of wisdom, all around,
In every laugh, a truth is found.
A sprinkle of chaos, a dash of cheer,
Life's recipe calls for guffaws, not fear.

Like mismatched socks that go their way,
I skip through puddles, come what may.
Collecting jokes like shiny stones,
In a mosaic that hums and moans.

Each day's a game of hide and seek,
With nonsense woven through the week.
So I dance along this quirky stream,
And toast to the madness—let's all dream!

Sculpting the Infinite

With humor carved in marble veins,
I shape my thoughts like rubber trains.
Chiseling life, each quirky line,
Turns out I'm the punchline divine.

Molding dreams from clouds of fluff,
The universe sighs, "That's enough!"
I sculpt my fears into paper cranes,
And giggle at my silly gains.

I've built a statue from my doubt,
Its nose too big, but what's that about?
A masterpiece with eyes aglow,
Winks at me with a friendly blow.

So here I stand, embracing chance,
In this sculpture's silly dance.
Life's a gallery of absurd delight,
And I'm the artist, try as I might.

Threads of the Cosmos

In a cafe, sipping my tea,
I ponder the stars and what they see.
Are they laughing or just so far,
Thinking of me like a little star?

A squirrel runs by, with a nut in tow,
I think, does he know more than we do, though?
Is he pondering life as he climbs that tree,
Or just plotting to eat for a nutty spree?

We dance on this planet, oh what a show,
With socks on our feet, ready to go.
While lost in a maze of old pizza crust,
Are we seekers of wisdom, or just filled with rust?

So here's to the questions, silly and vast,
Why do we worry about the future and past?
Let's laugh at the cosmos, we're here for the ride,
With mismatched socks and humor as our guide.

A Quest for Illumination

I woke up today with a quest in mind,
To uncover the truth that's so hard to find.
With a flashlight and donut, my tools of choice,
I'll solve all of life's puzzles, rejoice!

I tripped on the rug, oh what a delight,
As I pondered the meaning of wrong and right.
Does the cat in the window know what's amiss?
Or is she just plotting her next napping bliss?

With coffee and dreams, I scribble it down,
My theories on why feathers fall from the crown.
I ask my goldfish for wisdom and grace,
He just swims in circles, a lost little face.

So here's to our journey, absurd and fun,
With giggles and laughter until we are done.
Embrace all the chaos, let's light up the dark,
With silly discoveries igniting the spark.

Beyond the Wordless Silence

In the quiet of night, I hear a soft croak,
Is it the meaning or just a wise frog joke?
Hopping through cosmos, he's asking me, why?
I shrug and ask back, is that cake in the sky?

With socks mismatched and thoughts askew,
I ponder the wisdom of bubblegum blue.
Could the moon be laughing at our daily grind?
Or just a big rock, with no thoughts in mind?

A dance with the shadows, I twirl with glee,
Is life a grand show just for you and me?
If I wear my hat tilted, will wisdom ensue?
Or just a few chuckles from the critters who chew?

So I gather my dreams and twinkle my toes,
With a pinch of absurd, wherever life goes.
In the depths of the unknown, I dive and I dip,
Finding joy in the journey, a cosmic trip!

Tuning into the Unfathomable

With a radio made of macaroni and cheese,
I tune into galaxies, feeling the breeze.
Do the stars have a playlist, or just white noise?
Are they grooving to tunes or playing with toys?

I asked a wise turtle, who stopped by the pond,
He shook his shell slowly, of wisdom he's fond.
"Life's just a jigsaw, pieces askew,
But put it together, find what's true to you!"

I tried to catch thoughts on a butterfly's wing,
With a net full of laughter, I'd discovered a fling.
But the butterfly giggled and flew out of reach,
Saying, "Keep trying hard, there's wisdom to teach!"

So let's waltz through this weird little game,
Chasing after answers with no hint of fame.
In joy and confusion, let's dance on our feet,
For the fun of existence is oh so sweet!

Chasing Shadows of Purpose

In a room full of mirrors, I search for my style,
The more that I look, the more I beguile.
With socks on my hands and a hat on my knee,
I'm lost in the closet—what's next? A spree?

I dance with the dust bunnies, twirl in the sun,
They whisper sweet secrets—oh, isn't this fun?
I seek out the answers, but they play hide and seek,
While I'm here in my jammies, feelin' quite chic.

I wrote a great novel, it's all on a napkin,
Just need a translator—oh, where's my captain?
The ship is a rubber duck, sailing away,
With a crew of my dreams, it's time for a play!

As shadows grow longer and lunch turns to night,
I ponder existence, but it's quite a fright.
With pizza to ponder and jokes that won't quit,
I laugh at my journey, a ridiculous skit.

In Search of Stardust

I chased a bright comet, but tripped on my shoe,
Floated past planets, where laughter is due.
Each star is a giggle, each moon represents fun,
But I ended up dancing with clouds on the run.

Around every corner, I find a new quest,
To find joy and wonder—where's my treasure chest?
My map's full of doodles, my compass is spun,
But who needs directions when you're on the run?

Stardust is everywhere, sprinkled on toast,
A sprinkle of humor is what I love most.
I tried counting wishes, but lost track at three,
Instead, I just chuckle and laugh with a spree.

In this cosmic ballet, I trip on a grin,
With a wink and a nod, I embrace where I've been.
So here's to adventure, absurd and sublime,
In search of the stardust, I dance out of time.

Threads of Destiny

I wove a great tapestry, bright colors and blur,
Stitch by funny stitch, it's more chaos than spur.
A cat with a knitting needle, swirling around,
Unravels my yarn while I'm lost in my sound.

Each thread tells a story, but most are a joke,
Like a sock with a hole, or a donut—who woke?
I ponder the colors, and chuckle with glee,
At this quilt of confusion, it all seems to be.

Around every corner, there's yarn that I find,
Piles of good laughter—oh, what's on my mind?
I knit and I purl, but the stitches run wild,
With giggles like echoes, I'm my own child.

Threads of my journey weave tales full of jest,
In the fabric of living, I feel truly blessed.
So pass me the yarn, let's roll it up tight,
For I'm weaving this laughter, from dawn until night.

Unraveled Journeys

I set out on travels with maps made of dreams,
But GPS laughs, twists all my schemes.
With ducks that give directions in feathers and quacks,
I wander the roads marked by giggles and snacks.

In fields full of daisies, I trip on my feet,
A stumble becomes a new dance on the street.
Where flowers tell secrets and rabbits wear hats,
I lose all my worries and time with the chats.

I started with purpose, but oh where's my goal?
With each silly hiccup, I'm finding my soul.
The journey's the punchline, the laughter the prize,
In a world full of quirks, it's where the fun lies.

So here's to the missteps, the slips, and the dives,
I'm crafting my tale, where whimsy thrives.
On this path of the silly, I skip and I prance,
For livin' it fully is the best off-chance!

www.ingramcontent.com/pod-product-compliance
Lightning Source LLC
Chambersburg PA
CBHW051640160426
43209CB00004B/734